T0016207

I Deserve ALL the TReaTs

CAT AFFIRMATIONS
for Health, Happiness, and World Domination

Jennifer Calvert   Illustrated by Malgorzata Detner

CASTLE POINT BOOKS
NEW YORK

I Deserve All the Treats.
Copyright © 2023 by St. Martin's Press.
All rights reserved. Printed in China.
For information, address St. Martin's Publishing Group,
120 Broadway, New York, NY 10271.

www.castlepointbooks.com

The Castle Point Books trademark is owned by Castle Point Publishing, LLC.
Castle Point books are published and distributed by St. Martin's Publishing Group.

ISBN 978-1-250-28714-4 (paper over board)
ISBN 978-1-250-28715-1 (ebook)

Design by Joanna Williams

Our books may be purchased in bulk for promotional, educational,
or business use. Please contact your local bookseller or the Macmillan
Corporate and Premium Sales Department at 1-800-221-7945, extension 5442,
or by email at MacmillanSpecialMarkets@macmillan.com.

First Edition: 2023

10 9 8 7 6 5 4 3 2 1

Dedicated to the loving memory of Boo,
the mild-mannered gentleman,
and to Cricket,
the little brother he never wanted.

—J.C.

The PUrFeCt TEacheR

IF YOU'VE EVER NOTICED A CAT SNORING PEACEFULLY in a warm swath of sunlight or staring deep into your soul at dinnertime and thought, *let's swap*, this is the book for you. Its pages hold the keys to that whiskered wisdom, that catlike confidence, that feline joie de vivre that inspires envy and commands respect from creatures great and small.

Who better to turn to for advice than the most adorably self-assured creatures in history? Cats take ownership of their lives. And your life. And the bed. And that screw you needed to stabilize the dresser. These diminutive descendants of lions and tigers know better than anyone who they are, what they're worth, and how to enjoy themselves.

Like their favorite spot on the couch, they won't share their secrets willingly. But careful observation and the occasional shameless bribe can reveal their ancient ways. *I Deserve All the Treats* distills that tuna-induced insight into simple affirmations you can use to become happier, healthier, and haughtier. (Because, if we've learned anything from cats, it's that you can tumble sideways into the dishwasher at full speed and still keep your head held high.)

With just a few minutes of practice each day, you'll learn how to establish boundaries, enjoy complete independence while relying on others for everything, make time for self-care, get revenge on your enemies, and so much more. Embrace the furry logic and four-legged poise that have helped cats thrive for thousands of years, and you'll find yourself feeling calm, confident, and ready to take on (or over) the world in no time!

I am the ruler
of my domain.

I am worthy
of the best
life has to offer.

My dreams
are powerful.

I decide
who gets the privilege
of my company.

Being willing
to change my mind
is a strength.

I stand up for myself
when I'm mistreated.

Joy comes
in many forms.

I prioritize self-care.

My inner light
shines brightly.

I make time
for movement
I enjoy.

I am a
generous friend.

Water replenishes
and refreshes me.

I am a
problem solver.

Focusing on my goal
ensures my success.

I face
my fears
head on.

I honor my
personal boundaries.

My instincts
serve me well.

I meet each moment
with grace.

I am open to
going wherever
my curiosity
takes me.

My worth
doesn't depend
on my work.

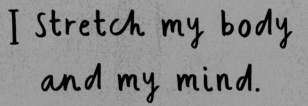

I stretch my body
and my mind.

I protect what's important to me.

My love and affection
lift up those I care about.

I see through
the darkness.

I communicate my needs
when I'm upset.

The food I eat
fuels me.

I am the
main attraction.

New beginnings
excite me.

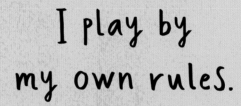

I play by
my own rules.

I live in the
present moment.

Opportunities to play
present themselves often.

I am happy to ask for help
when I need it.

The beauty of nature nourishes me.

A fresh perspective
changes everything.

I create space
for rest.

I am constantly learning.

I pause
to appreciate
how far
I've come.

Those who love me
support my goals.

I remember to pace myself
in all endeavors.

Flexibility is
my Superpower.

I release what doesn't serve me.

I am worthy
of adoration.

Not every mess
is mine to clean up.

I greet the morning with unbridled enthusiasm.

I deserve all the treats.

Feeling stuck
is temporary.

I am my own
best advocate.

I give myself
permission to feel
what I need to feel.

The glass is as full
as I choose to see it.

I am a
divine being.

I leave my mark
on the world.

There is beauty
in chaos.

I am the master
of my universe.

Jennifer Calvert is an author, editor, and all-around book-loving nerd who befriends furry creatures wherever she goes. Throughout her life, cats have been a constant source of love, inspiration, mild irritation, and joy. She currently serves a mischievous orange-and-white tabby at her home in New Jersey.

Malgorzata Detner is a Poland-based illustrator with a lifelong love of art. Influenced by old animation, Malgorzata's favorite things to draw are mysterious, fantastic worlds and creatures of all kinds in vibrant colors. She currently lives with her family, a cocker spaniel, snails, and two lovely rats in Warsaw.